# Project Planning Checklist

by David Locicero
architect

Oakland, California

©2016, David Locicero, architect. All rights reserved.
DSLociceroarchitect.com

## Project Planning Checklist

## Table of Contents

Introduction ............................................................. 5

General Information .............................................. 9

Property Information ........................................... 13

Alteration Plans ..................................................... 15

Budgeting ................................................................ 17

Finding + Selecting an Architect ....................... 23

Final Thoughts ...................................................... 29

About The Author ................................................. 31

## Project Planning Checklist

# Introduction

Thinking about remodeling or adding on to your home can be an overwhelming experience. There are so many issues and so many details. There are design issues, construction issues, budgeting issues, building codes and so much more. Where should you start?

Start at the beginning!

Before you or your architect can even begin to think about those issues, some basic information is required.

I prepared this Checklist for use in my own architectural practice during initial meetings with my clients. It provides me and my clients with a single document to record the critical information about their projects.

These same questions are often asked by my clients before they hire an architect. Consequently, I expanded the checklist to include sections about determining a construction budget, and finding and selecting an architect.

If you follow this checklist through to the end you will have all the information your architect will need to kick off the project in the best possible way. Even if you can't find all the information, you will be significantly more prepared than most.

David Locicero
Architect

# Project Planning Checklist

## Project Planning Checklist

## General Information

☐ Project Address

_____

_____

_____, California _____

☐ Jurisdiction:
The jurisdiction will be the City you live in, or if you live in an unincorporated area, the County you live in.

_____

Most of the information about the Assessors Parcel Number, Block Number, Lot Number, and Zoning district will be available from your Jurisdiction's Planning Department. The Residence Type should be self-evident. If not the Building Department can tell you.

☐ Assessors Parcel Number:
_____

The APN is a unique number used by the County Assessor to identify your property. It is different from your address. The APN is often required when you apply for a permit.

☐ Block Number:

_____

The Block Number is an identifier used in some Cities, particularly San Francisco, to locate a property in the official maps of the City. The Block Number is often required when you apply for a permit.

☐ Lot Number:

_____

The Lot number is an identifier used in conjunction with the Block Number in some cities, particularly San Francisco, to locate a property in the official maps of the City. The Lot Number is often required when you apply for a permit.

☐ Zoning:

_____

# Project Planning Checklist

- Residence Type:
    - Single Family – Detached
    - Single Family – Attached
    - Multi-family – Condominium
    - Multi-family – Tenants-in-common

# Project Planning Checklist

## Property Information

☐ Lot Size:

_____

☐ Lot Area:

_____

☐ Existing House Area:

_____

☐ Number of stories:

_____

☐ Building height:

_____

☐ Existing Set Backs:

The existing set backs will be compared with the code required/allowed set backs to determine the extent to which your property can be expanded.

☐ Front Set Back: _____

☐ Back Set Back: _____

☐ Side Set Back (left): _____

☐ Side Set Back (right): _____

## Project Planning Checklist

## Alteration Plans

☐ Identify the nature of the problem you are solving. Is the problem about:

- ☐ lack of light?
- ☐ not enough storage?
- ☐ difficult circulation patterns?
- ☐ insufficient space?
- ☐ something else?

_____

_____

_____

☐ Are you planning to:
- ☐ Remodel (internal changes only)
- ☐ Add on (expanding the area of the house)
    - ☐ Adding a New floor or level
    - ☐ Expanding into the yard
    - ☐ Enclose a garage
    - ☐ Enclose a porch
    - ☐ Develop the basement
    - ☐ Develop the back of the garage (San Francisco Marina Style houses)

☐ What spaces are being remodeled (altered)?
- ☐ Kitchen
- ☐ Bath
- ☐ Master Bath
- ☐ Other – List:

_____

_____

_____

☐ What spaces are being added?
- ☐ Master Bedroom
- ☐ Bedroom
- ☐ Office/Study
- ☐ Kitchen
- ☐ Bath
- ☐ Master Bath
- ☐ Other – List:

_____

_____

# Project Planning Checklist

## Budgeting

**Available Funds:**

☐ Are you planning on living in the house during construction?
    ☐ Yes

    Are you sure about that?
    If you are remodeling you Kitchen, budget more for food during construction – there will be take out.

    ☐ No

    Where will you live during construction?

    _____

    Have you budgeted for the expense?

    _____


☐ What is your budget?

$ _____

If you have money set aside, or are procuring financing, I recommend the following breakdown of expenses:

A. Total available budget:

$ _____

B. Reserve 10% for unexpected expenses: (Total x 0.10 = reserve):

$ _____

C. Allow up to 15% for plan check, permits, and other fees: (Total x 0.15 = city fees):

$ _____

D. Allow 15% for architects/engineers fees (for residential work this will vary from 10% to 20% depending on the size and complexity of the project. Small projects are not necessarily less expensive than large projects.):
(Total x 0.15 = prof. Services):

$ _____

# Project Planning Checklist

E. Are you living off-site during construction? Allow some money for this:

$ _____

F. Add the Reserve number, the city fees number and the professional services number. These are the "soft costs".
From above: B + C + D + E =

$ _____

Subtract the soft costs from the total available budget. This is your actual construction budget.
A – F = Actual Construction Budget:

$ _____

**Likely Construction Costs:**

☐ Will your construction budget be sufficient for your project?

The following information is from HomeAdvisor.com.

Note that the amounts below are AVERAGE costs. It is possible to build for less, though if you want nicer finishes, it is very easy to spend more.

*Average National Costs Per Square Foot:*

- *Interior painting: $3.40/Sq.Ft. of floor area*
- *Install hardwood floor: $7.32/Sq.Ft.*
- *Window replacement: $405/window*
- *New addition without plumbing: $100 - $150*
- *With bathroom: $125 - $200*
- *With kitchen: $250 - $300*
- *With both: $250 - $350*
- *New deck with steps and rails: $20 - $30*

*Here are the national price averages and ranges for different remodel projects:*

- *Kitchens - $19,420*
- *Bathrooms - $7,830*

# Project Planning Checklist

In my experience, costs in the San Francisco Bay Area will run <u>at least</u> **20% higher than the amounts shown above.**

For a description of San Francisco Bay Area construction costs see this web page: http://www.remodeling.hw.net/cost-vs-value/2016. Select the Pacific region. Once that is done you can select your city, or a very near one from the list. This will take you to a page where you can download their report once you've provided some information.

☐ Estimating your construction costs.

    ☐ Calculate the floor area of your remodel or addition. The floor area is the Width x the Length:
width _____ x length _____ = _____square feet

    ☐ Multiply the floor area, calculated above, time the construction costs listed above. If the exact project type is not listed use the one most like what you have planned.
Floor area _____ x construction cost _____ = $_____

☐ Compare your construction budget from page 19 with your estimated project cost above.

☐ Is your budget larger than the estimated project cost?

☐ Yes. Move on to finding an architect.

☐ No. Consider your options:

> ☐ Can the project area be smaller?
> ☐ Are less expensive finishes acceptable to you?
> ☐ What are your priorities? What is most important? Can you reduce the scope of the project?
> ☐ Can your objectives be achieved with a smaller project size?
> ☐ Can your objectives be achieved over time in several incremental or phased projects?

Often an architect or contractor can help you sort out these questions in one or two meetings. But be prepared to compromise.

# Project Planning Checklist

## Finding + Selecting An Architect

☐ Ask your family, friends or acquaintances for referrals to architects they have used. Find out their website addresses. You can do this by Googling their names or calling them and asking.

☐ Do an internet search for architects in your area with your project type as one of the search terms (Remodel, Kitchen Remodel, Addition, Modern, Small space design, or whatever you need.)

☐ Check sites like Houzz.com or Servicemagic.com.

☐ Check the websites of the first 10 or so names you get as referrals and internet search results.
    ☐ Do you like the work you see?
    ☐ Do you like the way they write about their firm and their work?

☐ Narrow your list down to 2 or 3 and contact them by phone or email and quickly describe your project and ask if they take on projects like yours. Mention how you got their name, especially if was through a referral.

☐ If they say "yes", set up an appointment to meet them. I prefer to do this meeting at the prospective client's house so I can see the site and house. Other architects prefer to do this meeting in their offices. Some architects will charge you for this initial meeting. Ask if there is a cost associated with this meeting and how much it will be.

☐ If they say they can't take on your project, ask them if they know a colleague who does take on projects like yours whom they might recommend.

☐ Talk to a couple of architects.

☐ Ask how they work. What is their process like?

☐ Ask them to describe their "style".

☐ Describe your problem to them and what you are thinking of doing.

☐ Tell them what your total budget is and what your construction budget is.

☐ Ask them to what extent they will be involved in your project? Many architects have staff who will be involved. You want to know if the person you are interviewing is a figurehead or "in the trenches".

☐ If you don't know, ask them if they have done work

# Project Planning Checklist

in your city.

☐ If they bring a portfolio or brochure, look through it and listen to how they describe the projects and the experiences with the clients.

☐ Ask them for references.

☐ **Do you like them? Do you "hit it off"? Are they pretentious? Do they seem bossy?**

☐ After you have spoken with several architects, call one or two back and ask them for a proposal. If you are getting proposals from more than one architect, let them know.

☐ When you receive the proposal, let them know you have received it and when you will be making your decision.

☐ Review the proposal(s). Are you looking at Apples and Oranges, or Apples and Apples?

☐ Does their description of your projects sound like they understood what you really want?

☐ Do they include the same services?

☐ Do they exclude any services?

☐ Do they include a proposed schedule?

☐ How is it structured? Hourly? Time + Expenses? Flat Fee? Percent of Construction Cost? Some mixture of these?

Remember, the proposal is just that, a proposal. If you don't feel comfortable with their description of your project, if you feel the schedule is wrong, if you feel there are too many, or not enough services included, or if their compensation is too high for your budget, and you are really interested in working with the architect, let them know. Discuss it with them. Ask them to revise their proposal.

☐ Select your architect based on:

　　☐ Do you like and trust this person?

　　Working with an architect is kind of intimate in that you will be discussing your hope and dreams and finances and how you really live. You need to be comfortable with whoever you select.

# Project Planning Checklist

☐ Do you like the work they've done in the past?
Do you think you they can listen to what you say and adjust appropriately?

☐ Are you comfortable with their proposal, their services, schedule and compensation?

☐ Sign an agreement / contract with your selected architect. In California, a contract must include the following to be "binding":

☐ A description of the services – what the architect will do.
☐ A schedule – when the architect will do it.
☐ The compensation – what you will pay the architect and when.
☐ Names + signatures of both parties.

☐ I also think an agreement / contract should include the following (though not required by law):

☐ A description of the project, project goals
☐ A description of the owner's responsibilities
☐ A termination clause that works both ways
☐ What happens if there are changes to the project or schedule.

☐ Understanding that drawings are not products but "instruments of service", tools used by the architect to describe the design to the city and contractor.

## Project Planning Checklist

## Final Thoughts

Now that you have completed this check list, you have:

☐ the critical information about your house and lot

☐ the start of an idea of how to solve the design problem

☐ preliminary thoughts about the total budget and the construction budget

☐ and an architect who will be working with you.

From this point on your architect will be working with you and will be leading you through the processes of programming, schematic design, design development, construction documents, permits, bidding, and construction.

Good luck!

Project Planning Checklist

## About The Author

David Locicero, architect, heads a San Francisco Bay Area based boutique architectural studio. David specializes in transforming problem houses into dream homes. He is also skilled at designing Accessory Dwelling Units (Granny Flats), kitchen and bath remodels, "Aging at home" solutions, as well as Code and accessibility consulting.

David brings his considerable experience on large, technologically complex buildings and construction administration to his passion for residential projects.

If you would like to talk to David about how he can help you with your project in California, he can be contacted through his website, dslociceroarchitect.com or by email at dslocicero@gmail.com.

Made in United States
Troutdale, OR
03/22/2025